To:

GAIL

with love

From:

Stevie

Thinking of You

By Pat Dickinson

Illustrated by Anne Smith

PETER PAUPER PRESS, INC.

White Plains, New York

Designed by Dawn DeVries Sokol

Illustrations copyright © 2001 Anne Smith/Lilla Rogers Studio

Text copyright © 2001
Peter Pauper Press, Inc.
202 Mamaroneck Avenue
White Plains, NY 10601
ISBN 0-88088-557-2
Printed in China
7 6 5 4 3 2 1

The very sight and sound

of you fills my sky with

sunshine

Every time I see you, it's like unwrapping a brand new gift.

Being with you is like
going to the circus,
wearing the ringmaster's
hat, and seeing sights no
one else knows are there.

When I'm at the end of my
rope, you send me down enough
life lines to lift me again
to a safe place.

You give me
more second chances
than one
person deserves.

You are my security blanket,
sheltering me with warmth,
kindness, and, even when
you don't understand,
empathy.

You help me find solutions,

or if there are none,

you help me bide my time

until they appear.

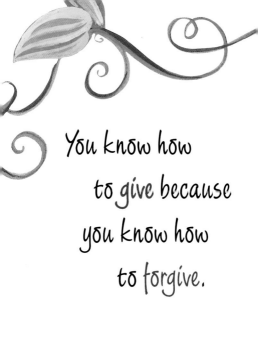

You know how
to give because
you know how
to forgive.

You always look long and far
enough to find the good in me.

You lift me up like a
thousand brightly colored
helium balloons against
a cloudless blue sky.

You make me
GLAD
I was born.

No matter how much time passes, we can start where we left off and, somehow, always grow.

The only predictable
thing about you is your
constant surprises.

When my heart is
heavy, you make my
soul soar on the
lightest of wings.

You make any

rain that falls

in my life

gentle and renewing.

You round the edges on

my sharp moments,

shaping my predicaments

into possibilities.

You know how to

treasure and keep

confidences.

Our days together are
never gray or dull because
YOU brighten all the
colors in my rainbow.

You do not boast

about your

accomplishments,

though they are many.

You know how to listen
with BOTH ears
and an open mind.

You appreciate the value
of time and make
every second count
for something.

You know how to slow down and appreciate all the flowers, not just the roses.

Remembering our good times together
brings a SMILE to my face,
peace to my mind,
and GRATITUDE to my heart.

You share your
GOODNESS
with everyone.
not just
a precious few.

You're as
comfortable on
a picnic as you
are in an elegant
restaurant.

You are caring when
I need caring and
tough when I need
toughening.

You never intentionally
harm any living thing,
and would not allow
anyone in your presence
to do so, either.

Your common sense is

worth a million bucks.

It feels GOOD

to see your face

in a crowd.

You are adventurous
and courageous enough
to walk through all the
doors of opportunity
that open before you.

You BELIEVE in
many things,
not the least
of which is me.

You recognize
KNOWLEDGE as the
only true power.

My feelings are important
to you and you guard them
graciously and generously.

You are a refuge,
a safe harbor in so many
of my personal storms.

You contribute to the
home, the community,
and the world in ways
too numerous to count.

You ENCOURAGE me
to discover the best
in myself and INSIST that
I search until I find it.

You CELEBRATE life
with a roar and complain
about its difficulties
in a whisper.

You hold onto your
dreams and make
me excited about
the possibility of
realizing mine.

Without knowing it, you have molded many lives by your honorable example.

You are not afraid to
make a mistake because
you recognize that's the
only way to become wiser.

The beauty on your face

when you SMILE rivals

any field of wild flowers

Your IMAGINATION
is boundless, and
you allow me to be
a frequent visitor.

You excel at untangling my troubles and weaving them into possibilities.

Because you
trust me, I am
able to trust
others.

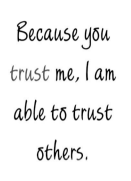

You MINIMIZE
my mistakes.

When we laugh
hysterically together,
all of nature joins in,
laughing right
along with us.

I'm glad you are so good at just being yourself and allowing me to just be me.

Because your world
revolves around others,
you don't even seem to
notice the shining star
that you are.

Your STRENGTH inspires
me to try to be strong.

Animals and children
like you because
they know a good
and gentle creature
when they see one.

Knowing you will always
be an important part of
my life brings daylight
to any dark moment.

You ALWAYS find the right words to say, and KINDLY leave the wrong words unspoken.

My wish for the world
would be a million more of you.

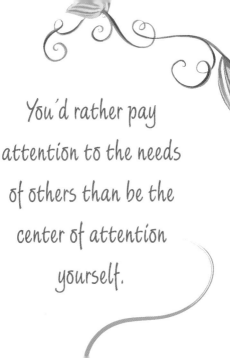

You'd rather pay
attention to the needs
of others than be the
center of attention
yourself.

My summer is sunnier,

my autumn more gold,

my winter more majestic,

and my spring more bold

because YOU season my life.

You have mastered reading
between the lines of my silence.

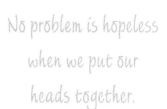

No problem is hopeless
when we put our
heads together.

You know when
to work hard and when
to play hard, valuing
the importance of both
in a balanced life

You know that money
isn't everything—
that the more you love,
the richer you become.

I am proud

of the person you

are and the person

I strive to be when I

am with you.

Time spent with
YOU is the best
part of any day.

You are patient and
strong at the very same time,
knowing that patience
amplifies strength.

I count my lucky stars

that we were placed in

the same universe.

You are responsible,
capable, dependable,
lovable, and just
plain able.

Your compassion knows no bounds
and you offer it willingly.

In this game of life,
every day that dawns
finds YOU a champion.

Words fall short
when I try to describe
how **THANKFUL** I am to
have you in my life.